BIBLICAL CATALYSTS FOR SUCCESSFUL ONLINE BUSINESS WORKING FROM HOME

STEP BY STEP GUIDE TO HAVING SUCCESSFUL BUSINESS ONLINE FOR EVERYONE

By

STEPHEN I. 'SANMY

This book is written to provide competent, reliable and verifiable information on the subject matter within its content. The Author and Publisher is NOT rendering legal, financial or other professional advice. If you need any of the services of the professionals, seek any of them in your locality.

NOTE: Kings James Version of the Holy Bible is used through the content of this book.

TABLE OF CONTENT

1. Inspiration of the Almighty
2. Sustainable Online Businesses To Consider
3. Forming Business for Your Inspiration
4. Team Up for Growth of Your Online Business
5. Use Internet for Your Business Advantage
6. How to get Money to Grow Your Online Business
7. Determination and Persistency have their Dividends on Online Business
8. Protect Your Online Business Intellectual Property
9. Compliance with Business Laws and Regulations
10. Expand Your Online Business Globally

CHAPTER ONE

INSPIRATION OF THE ALMIGHTY

There is need for you to know from the onset that there is no way you can just start a business without having right inspiration. Most of the common products and services around us these days were fuelled by inspirations of some people. We shall consider what is meant by the inspiration of the Almighty.

The first time I came across the words 'inspiration of the Almighty' in the bible is Job chapter 32 verses 8 and 9 which says, *"But there is a spirit in man: and the inspiration of the Almighty giveth them understanding. Great men are not always wise: neither do the aged understand judgment."* These verses caught my attention then. I took time to study deeper on these two verses. Briefly, I wish you caught the in-depth understanding of how these two bible verses can help you grow your online business start-ups or businesses growth faster than expected.

The Spirit in Man

I believe that every man or mankind is endowed with spirit. How the man or woman uses the spirit within him or her is a factor of many circumstances. These circumstances are family background, society, level of education, influencers, and expositions among others. Your ideal online business comes from the circumstance that your spirit is exposed to.

For instance, Mark Zuckerberg was inspired the environment he was then to start Facebook on February 4, 2004 together with his inspired friends in the Harvard University. I believe these friends, Eduardo Saverin, Andrew McCollum, Dustin Moskovitz and Chris Hughes will remain happy to be part of successful invention by their friend, Mark.

In reality, you can see that the inspirational factors that aided Mark Zuckerberg to become successful in his online invention were factors within the university environment and his friends.

At this junction, I want you to pause and consider what you think you are inspired about in order to start or improve your online business or grow your business. I may not be able to answer for you accurately, but I can say, "Your spirit man helps you to become an online business person!"

Inspiration of the Almighty

The inspiration of the Almighty is different from the "spirit in man." The term inspiration of the Almighty, to me, means "exposition of secret thing from the Supernatural Being to the spirit of man." From this perspective, I am not pious, but I must let you know that if anyone receives inspiration from God, the Almighty, you have gotten great hidden secret that shall definitely help you to succeed in online business.

The inspiration of the Almighty is derived from different sources. Few of these sources are from the Holy Bible, direct communication to your spirit, circumstances around you and many others. For instance, bible in Genesis Chapter 30 verse 4 states that, *"Then Jacob separated the lambs, and made the flocks face toward the streaked and all the brown in the flock of Laban; but he put his own flocks by themselves and did not put them with Laban's flock."* I believed God inspired Jacob with the cross-breeding mechanism to prosper him even in his father-in-law's house.

You need to take breath out and let God give you His inspiration. Starting any business online without God's guidance or your personal interest, it may not help you to grow successfully. When you get inspiration of the Almighty, you have gotten reliable source to accelerate your online business growth. The inspiration of the Almighty shall give you UNDERSTANDING!

Understanding

To my knowledge, the "understanding" you get from the inspiration of the Almighty, gives you comprehensive insight to make good decision on your online business. With understanding of the Almighty, you will get clarity of purpose on what to do, how to do it and how to sustain it. Many online businesses are selling products or services are around us in the country and they are doing very fine. Get inspiration to start online business. When you get the inspiration of the Almighty, you will understand what to and how to do your online business in different ways. The distinctiveness of your inspiration to start online business I will call "INSPIRED INNOVATION!"

From our example, before Mark Zuckerberg came up with his inspired innovation called "Facebook", there were different modalities on how people were connecting socially, but his innovation birthed new ways of socializing and changed the general status quo. Today, Mark Zuckerberg has consistently for years made online socializing easier almost all over the world.

Mighty Idea

If the inspiration from the Almighty is given to you to start online business or online service, you shall surely understand how to do the online business. I mean you will be inspired on the ways to go about the mighty idea. I can made bold to say that if your inspiration is given by the Almighty, then you have gotten "mighty idea" with potential of making mighty impact successfully through on online business you are starting or you want to grow.

I will advise you to seek the inspiration of the Almighty before you start online business or to grow your existing online business. When you get it, don't think it doesn't follow the norms in the society as usual. I can assure you, if the inspiration is from the Almighty; your idea is mighty idea that will surely succeed. But that is not all. In the subsequent chapters in this book, you will see how you shall move your online business to higher success and make mighty impact profitably.

Great men are not always wise

"Great men are not always wise" is part of the bible reference early made above. Having great businesses and services all around us in this country doesn't mean that their founders were the wisest before they started, but today, we can say they are wise because of the impacts they are making in the business world.

How does this statement "great men are not always wise" concern your online business or ideas? The major concern is that you cannot grow your business sustainably without having understandings of how to go about turning your mighty idea to successful online business within short time. Therefore, I want you to pause at this stage and write down the online business you are inspired within you to start or how you want your online business to grow. Not just any business, but it must be the mighty idea gotten into your spirit man through the breath of the Almighty.

Starting online business has become and most search words online. You need to start online business that will sustain you profitably in years to come.

Staring Online Business Hints

It is imperative to state the hints on what starting online business entails generally. It requires that you study how the successful online entrepreneurs have succeeded; understanding of time and commitments required physically; and understanding of the market and competitions already established, if any, the desired area of online business.

Summary and Biblical Illustrations

1. Everybody in Jacob's family would have had many dreams, but Joseph's dream in the family was inspiration of the Almighty which didn't conform with norms of other family members' dream. Dream was what brought Joseph to limelight in Egypt to the essence that Pharaoh said, "And Pharaoh said unto his servants, Can we find such a one as this is, a man in whom the Spirit of God is? And Pharaoh said unto Joseph, Forasmuch as God

hath shewed thee all this, there is none so discreet and wise as thou art:

Thou shalt be over my house, and according unto thy word shall all my people be ruled: only in the throne will I be greater than thou." (Genesis chapter 41 verse 38 to 40).

2. David was small lad among Jesse's sons but she got to the throne, though with many challenges. Imagine a teen-age boy saving a whole Nation from terror of a giant. The fact is that, the inspiration of the Almighty helped him.

In conclusion, if the inspiration of the Almighty fuels your business idea, it must be mighty idea that will have positive impacts on other persons' lives. That's to say, THE INSPIRATION OF THE ALMIGHTY BRINGS VALUABLE AND SUCCESSFUL CATALYSTS TO ANY BUSINESS.

CHAPTER TWO

SUSTAINABLE ONLINE
BUSINESSES TO CONSIDER

The bible states about the children of Issachar in the book of 1 Chronicles chapter 12 verse 32 as children, *"...Which were men that had understanding of the times, to know what Israel ought to do; the heads of them were two hundred; and all their brethren were at their commandment."* These bible references are important for us in this chapter. Think about the economic situation of every family in U.S. or in any country in the world. You will agree with me that there is need for every one of us to **understand the time** we are! It is the time when your income, my income or a family income is not enough to meet up with the pressing needs financially.

The bible reference above tells us that the children of Issachar know what Israel ought to do! I believe too that what you ought to do is to start online business and enjoy financial freedom in years to come instead of waiting for government welfare packages or pay income that is not enough.

I am not condemning welfare packages or our income from our current income from our jobs. But you and I need extra or total source of income online that is sustainable for years to come.

If you understand the time we are in now with the current trends in the world, you will agree with me that there is need to make more reliable incomes from online business. Why?! More people, regardless of age grades, buy and pay for products online comfortably from any where there provided they are connected with the internet.

In chapter one, I told you that you need to be guided by the inspiration of the Almighty to know which mighty idea you can turn to business. I will try to discuss few online businesses that I believe to be sustainable for a while if one tap their potentials now. There may be more online businesses, but I will briefly discuss highly demanding online businesses all over the world today.

15 Sustainable Online Businesses You can Start Today

1. Graphic Designing: Have you ever thought why businesses use different logos, design and graphic pictures for their goods, services and branding? The open secret is that business persons use these graphic designing to establish their businesses. What is graphic design? One can say that is the act of designing visual, graphical and coloring to pass across salient points to the public. If are good at this skill, you will certainly make good income from online business. Every day, businesses seek the services of graphic designer to create concepts for their business logos, website designing, product designing, and concept pictorial creation among other uses.

If you are skillful in graphic designing, congratulations to you. Get to work and start making money through the skill online. If you are interested without the skill of graphic designing, you can actually learn the skill from many online teaching platforms or online training through some universities online programs for few weeks.

I am convinced that this online business will be relevant for years to come because more businesses will always seek how to design many creative crafts to promote their goods, services and brand.

2. Virtual/Online Instructing: This skill has made every willing person to become virtual instructor online and decent income is made through this. Why? No matter whom you are and where you are, if you can read this book to this page, I believe you are great instructor! Yes, there are some things you are naturally good at or that you have learnt years back. The skill can be online business to you and this will surely bring more income to you if you are tenacious to make it great from this online business.

You will agree with me that when the pandemic of Corona Virus caused the governments to take the policy of staying at home to reduce the spread of the pandemic, more people in their homes used the opportunity to learn online paid courses or free download as a lead to buying other product or service from instructors.

You will be surprised that many people are ready to learn anything online. Let me list few things, though not exhaustive, that people seek to learn online: How to plan for wedding; how to make money online; how to become better me; how to build my love for my spouse; how to stay health always; how to train your dogs; how to swim; how to reduce fat; how to cook certain food, how to... how to...etc!

This will be a sustainable business for years to come since internet is available to everyone.

3. *Data Analysis*: This requires learning the system before you can make money online through it. There are many businesses, organizations and institutions who are seeking expert to analyze their data in order to make informed decisions.

4. *Online Interior/exterior decoration*: This is a huge business for anyone that can see gold in it. Interior decoration for houses, offices and events are becoming huge business online. More also, exterior decoration can fetch anybody who knows his/her technical how to present the business online.

5. *Web and Application Developments*: More businesses and organizations will always want to develop new or old

websites or applications for their businesses or object-ives. You can learn this skill and create Business Empire for yourself. This is a sustainable business that will last for years to come. More applications and websites will be needed for the new upcoming businesses or institu-tional demands.

6. *Crypto Currency Consulting*: You may be wondering how this can be a sustainable business. I believe there is still more relevance for crypto currencies in future. I believe they will come back booming in years to come. How do you then make money online through crypto curren-cies? You can make money through writing facts about it, you can invest for future boom, you can mine the cur-rencies and you can become a consultant online if you know the detail requirements and news around the fu-ture of crypto currencies.

7. *Deep Learning Analytical Consulting*: Deep learning ana-lytical consulting is a novel ways of making very huge from now. This is a system that stems from machine learning which is also referred to as artificial intelligence (AI) application consulting. AI systems are becoming great tools for everyone online now. By pro-gramming data, AI will, by default, automatically learn and improve their capacity from the programmed de-veloped earlier without necessarily creating new pro-gramming. If you learn this system and become an ex-pert on it, soon you will be making handsome some of dollars!

8. *Online Events Planning*: Many people want to know where and when some events are coming up; while some businesses or organizations want to organize certain events in the future but they may not be able to reach much audience. If you create your website and start on-

line business in this niche, you will see that soon, your website will become the home of event panning. I may not be able to explain to you in detail. But you can just think around this. If there is a great event in Texas in the next summer which will benefit some categories of people, if the event is placed on your website for a token, you get more traffic for your website and attract more advertisement revenue.

9. *Online Book Writing and Punishing*: This has made everyone who is good at writing any kind of genre to become bestseller author within short time. The online book stores like Amazon, Createspace, among others have made writing easy. If you write your book on any of the online marketing book stores. Your books can be sold in major countries in the world in hard copies, audio format and eBook format. If you are prolific writer, you can write on the areas of your knowledge or you can outsource your book's writing to competent freelancer or ghost writers. When you start doing this online publishing and you keep on writing steadily, you will continue to make sustainable income from years to come if your books are relevant.

You can start selling your books on your website without sharing profits with any other persons except your affiliates.

10. *Blogging*: Blogging has been here for a while and it will still be a sustainable means of incomes for as many who will tap to the opportunities embedded in blogging business. The important thing about blogging is for you to stick with your passion on your blog's contents. You build your blog with traffic and soon, your blog will soon become authority blog to refer to I the niche you focus on.

11. *Online Sales Platform*: This is a website that you set up as business to help both sellers and buyers to meet on your website to buy and sell. Ebay.com has been most

successful e-commerce website in U.S. today with millions of buying and selling transactions monthly. You can set up your online business in this line too and make sustainable incomes for years to come.

12. **Online Forum**: Online forum has been around for years now; it will still be relevant online business for years to come. Why? This because people always reach out to forum to learn from different people with like-minded persons in a forum. You can start this business small but grow to empire of great business with huge potential of incomes in the nearest future.

13. ***Selling and Buying Domain Names***: Buying and selling of domain names is good business to start easily online with huge opportunity of making money online. But this business requires understanding what is require for you to succeed greatly in the business. You must take time to conduct research on names that are relevant to current events around the world or your immediate environment. You can start domain name sales or business from today from Godaddy.com, name.com. Dynadot.com, etc.

14. **Online Tourism Consulting:** Tourism is billion dollars' industry in the world. You cannot regret if you start this business and do it with competent hands. Just make your online tourism consulting know through thorough.

In conclusion, don't just kick starts online business without taking precautionary steps. You should search from your heart and get God's inspiration on what exactly is the business you should start online.

CHAPTER THREE

FORMING BUSINESS FROM THE MIGHTY INSPIRATION

In this chapter, we shall take steps further to consider how to form business from the mighty inspiration I consider in chapter one above. Forming business from the mighty inspiration involves basic concepts enumerate below:

1. **Legality**: Business to be formed from any inspiration from the Almighty must be one that is legally permitted in the state or country that you live. Note, God is not author of confusion, I believe He will not give you mighty inspiration that is against the law of the land. If the inspiration is not legal, I will say it is not a mighty idea.

2. **Value:** Forming business from mighty inspiration indicates that there's value to consumers, clients a customers. Essence of mighty inspiration is to help humanity to overcome challenges or problems.

3. **Purpose**: The business must have purpose and meet the purpose for the targeted audience.

4. **Capacity**: Is the business owner has the capacity physically, materially, financially and emotionally to form the business received from mighty inspiration.

5. **Identification of Retailers/End-user**.

6. **Sustainability**: The business should have self-sustaining strength by its forms and distribution of products or services.

7. **Longevity**: The business should have capability to live longer and for a constant period. Although it may not be forever.

With the above basic concepts, you have to take proactive measure to form the business. Everybody knows that forming a business involves your State office for business or company incorporation. Most importantly, the nature of your business idea and objectives of its operation determine type of business you will have to incorporate. Note that most of the business corporations and limited liability companies (LLC) are incorporated in order to protect the business owner(s) from personal liability antecedent to incurred debts, taxations and business legal matters

As a start-up, the choice of your incorporation is your sole responsibility. If you have incorporated your business already, kudos to you! But I must make it clear that most start-ups prefer to incorporate businesses on the LLC status due to its flexibility and other advantages. It is imperative to let you know that advantages and disadvantages of any mode of business you incorporate generally relate to:

a.   Liability from costs and other financial responsibilities and business legal matters;

b.   Prohibitions or restrictions on number of the business ownership;

c.   Ability to transfer stockholding or ownership to other person or entity;

d.   Ability to invite public to subscribe to the company stock or shareholding;

e.   Banking and contract matters;

f.   Costs of incorporation of the business which is relative to which state you are incorporating the business and

g.   State's legal control compliance on corporate governance of the business.

Generally, forming a business entity is important for everyone who is venturing to make money as business person. So, your business formation based on the mighty inspiration you have gotten gives your business legal entity with many benefits from other businesses, customers, clients and the state or the country at large.

The Diagram blow shows the summary of Business Corporations you can start legally in the U.S. or any part of the world subject to various laws in the jurisdictions of the other countries.

LIMITED LIABILITY COMPANY (LLC)	CONVENTIONAL CORPORATION	S CORPORATION	LIMITED PARTNERSHIP	PARTNERSHIP	SOLE PROPRIETORSHIP
Incorporation requires legal documentations	State Legally controlled on Incorporation. Good for big companies.	State incorporation with lesser requirements to C Corporation	State Incorporation legally required	Requires legal formation	Simple Procedure to start.
Taxed as entity	Taxed double with many legal commitments and corporate governance	Taxation Like in Sole Proprietorship	Double Taxations from personal and the entity.	Taxations is from personal income of partners	Taxation is from personal proprietor
Challenges and liability limited to the entity	Challenges faced are many	Challenges faced by owner(s)	Challenges of legal documentation and others are shared	Challenges are shared by partners	Challenges are carried by the sole proprietor
Two or more owners	More owners	One or more	Two or more owners	Two or more can for a partnership	One person can start the business

Most Start-ups have always been asking if it is necessary to start with Incorporation of their Companies immediately they want to commence their online business as special business with new idea. My advice is that you are not required to first go to state office to incorporate the business if you are not financially buoyant. Nevertheless, there is no way you can start some businesses which require licensing or other state's requirements. You must first find out details about the mighty inspiration you have received. Write the mighty idea down and follow the piece of advice on teaming up with some experts (if need be) in **Chapter 3** of this book. The team will guide you right on ways to go about your mighty business idea.

For instance, we have earlier considered how Mark Zuckerberg started facebook. Do you know that it took him days and weeks before he could set up the company up as a corporation? Your mighty idea may not be rushed to be incorporated as business online but must be thoroughly guided to avoid pitfalls that affect first start-ups to business world.

CHAPTER FOUR

TEAM UP FOR GROWTH OF
YOUR ONLINE BUSINESS

There is no one can succeed alone without the help of others. Your mighty inspiration to start online business or to move your business higher online successfully requires team up with relevant experts. The Holy Bible says in the multitude of counsel a city is built. To build a successful business, you need a team of counselors who are experts in their fields.

These team members that are needed to make you online business grow successfully are lawyer, tax advisor, financial experts, marketers, managerial board members, risk manger, etc.

These team members are essential to help you through of your online business. In Holy Bible, there are various examples of team members who helped leaders to achieve great feats at different locations and situations. Moses was burden of leading and judging the Israelites. Laban, Moses' father in law was a counselor and visionary adviser. Laban advised Moses and his advice was helpful to Moses on his leadership. Joseph told Pharaoh in the Holy Bible in Genesis chapter 41 verse 34 that Pharaoh should appoint officers over the land. These officers worked as a team to achieve great inspiration of Joseph business as Prime Minister in Egypt at that time.

If you study the life of the Lord Jesus Christ, He didn't worked alone but chose 12 disciples who worked and assisted His earthly ministry.

As you decide to choose your team members, you need these team members to help you accelerate your mighty business inspiration. We shall briefly consider few of them and how their expertise will assist you.

Lawyer: Lawyer is a veritable expert to guide you through statutory requirements for your online business to be incorporated with the state incorporation office; help you on all legal documentations; contract drafting, acquisitions of property, legal claims, intellectual property matters and other relevant functions. Are you thinking that lawyer fee is high for you? No, you won't regret having him or her to work for on your online business. There is another way which has reduced your cost on getting the services of lawyer and pay lesser fee. I will refer you to possible methods to explore to get cost effective means to hire a lawyer with competency in practice towards the end of this chapter.

Tax Advisor: Business that is statutory required to pay tax to the state or a country as the case may be are required to seek advice of tax advisor for guidance. There is need for you to have a skillful tax advisor who can help you through your online business payments of required taxes and midwives between your business and government on tax waiver for business, if need be. You may think this expert's fee may be too high for you, but tax advisor's advice and guidance will certainly help you to accelerate your online business success. There are also means to go about getting cheap but better tax advisor towards the end of this chapter.

Financial experts: These experts range from auditors, accountants and book keepers. An auditor helps you in auditing your business account. Accountants are also good at helping online business to grow sequel to their accounting skill for your income and expenditures periodically. Book keepers are good at making your financial book keeping in various ledgers are kept accurately.

Products or Service Marketers: Your products or services are not going to be known or reached the actual customers or clients if you don't engage marketers to help sell or promote your services online. There are better ways to have your online business to move on profitably without the marketers these days. If you are small business, Start-up, you don't need them now. But if your business is large enough you may need them to move your online business products or services.

Managerial board: You are part of this team. You may decide to have many like-minds persons to work as your team managers who will see to daily activities. When you operate with mighty idea of business inspiration, you need to keep books or ledgers in order to know the growth, stagnancy or retrogression of your operations so that you can make informed decisions periodically.

Risk Manager: There is common maxim that life is a risk. Every endeavor in life therefore is a risk. In lieu of this, there is no way one can have successful business of mighty inspiration without risk manager. Your risk manager helps mainly in the areas of insurance, security and safety of your business assets. A wise man will do everything to keep himself and household from danger. Likewise, a wise business owner will ensure to keep his or business from danger and unforeseen calamity.

NOTE AND RESOURCES
I will like you to consider the following online resources if you don't have enough capital to hire your team members. But note that I am not an affiliate to any of the online resources I am pointing your attention to here. Do your due diligence while dealing with the websites.

1. Check upwork.com; freelancer.com; fiverr.com; peopleperhour.com and truelancer.com among others.
2. On these websites, you can get most of your team members that will help you to accelerate your success in the business.

3. Don't just pick any freelancer on these websites; consider the number of years, jobs done, and feedbacks of clients they have worked with.
4. Compare carefully and give your job to any freelancer you have chosen. Give details of your expectation of the job or explain that you need expert and professional jobs to be done for you.
5. Yes, you will see professionals licensed in your state or country to do any of your desire job for you on any of the websites.

Summary and Biblical Illustrations

1. Bible discusses in the book of Ephesians chapter 4 verse 11 that Jesus empowered different people as a body of the mighty mission of reconciling the word to God. In doing that, he gave some, apostles; and some, prophets; and some, evangelists; and some, pastors and teachers." If you notice carefully with the scripture, you will see clearly that every great project like your mighty business requires good team members with their various skills and experience.

2. Another important factor to put into consideration is that the team members must have like-minds towards achieving same goals of successful mighty idea to be established as your business. See what the Bible says in the book of Romans chapter 15 verse 5 in order to ensure that one doesn't need to keep every Dick and Harry to be team members of a mighty business. The Scripture says, "Now the God of patience and consolation grant you to be like-minded one toward another according to Christ Jesus." Ensure that your team is like-minded towards your inspired mighty business.

3. There is a story of a middle aged man who got inspired

that there would be scarcity of grains for industries in the following years. He decided to go to a country side to lease 2 hectares of farmland to grow the grain. But he refused to neither hire nor invite anybody to work with him. Eventually, he couldn't realize his goal. Indeed, industries purchased grains at higher rates of over 1000% increase due to scarcity of grains.

If he had hired and used mechanized farming with advise of experts, he would have become a point of reference for the purchases of the grains during scarcity.

CHAPTER FIVE

USE INTERNET FOR YOUR
BUSINESS ADVANTAGE

An online business needs internet in this modern world. In this chapter, we are not strictly discussing what we discussed in chapter three above on freelancer websites, but I will guide you into details of how you can use internet to expand and move your mighty idea forward successfully.

Aims and Objectives of Your Online Business

The inspiration of the Almighty which is fuelling the online business you are starting or you are about to reinforce demands for clarity of purpose. Please, get time to write down in detail the aims and objectives of the inspiration you have received. Holy Bible says in the book of Habakkuk chapter 2 verse 2 that, "And the LORD answered me, and said, Write the vision, and make it plain upon tables, that he may run that readeth it." Your aims and objectives are like the business plan that guides you to know the factors needed to forge ahead. These factors include, but not limited to, your business mission, areas of expansion, business model, model to overcome competitions, operational guide, model to actualize realistic progress, model to overcoming business challenges among other salient factors.

There are various applications or software with programs on business planning, modeling in order to achieving set down aims and objectives. Use Google to search for these applications.

Get a Website for Your Online Business

It will be understatement if I tell you that most businesses may not be able to succeed these days without a website to reach out to wider people that may need the businesses' products or services. Let us imagine that you are travelling with your car from New York City to Washington DC which close to almost five hours' journey and you decides to find out a mechanic along the road, what will you do? Sure! You will definitely search and locate one online along your ways. That is the power of information technology to enhance your business and all that you do.

Getting website for your business has become so easier that you can get it done within minutes. The first thing to do first is to get your Domain Name first.

Getting Your Domain Name

Your business domain name is very important to your mighty business inspiration. If, for instance, your business idea is about making a unique soap for pets, then you may need a short domain name like- uniquepetsoap, petsoap, bestpetsoap etc. The true is that, you have to search from the common domain name registries and market places like godaddy.com, uniregistry.com, sedo.com, dynadot.com, name.com, namesilo.com among others. The next important factor to bear in mind is the extension you choose for your domain name. The extension- (.com), (.org), (.net), (.co),etc are the common domain name extensions. But the common one for commercial purpose is (.com) extension which is most popular in the world and it has gain vantage position among other extension.

I encourage you to make your domain name a short one with (.com) extension. You have to make sure that your domain name is not infringing on the other business trademark or intellectual property. For instance, you cannot say your desire domain name is nike.com, you cannot get the domain, if at all you got the domain, you will definitely be faced for claims from the trademarked domain. (You will know much about your business intellectual property and rights in chapter 7 of this book).

Building Your Business Website

Building your business website can be done from many domain name registries within minutes with what is called- What You See Is What You Get (WYSIWG) or Do-It-for-You (DIY). You will have it done and you take control of your website. The essential demarcations on your website are shown on the website bar, which are: Home Page; Products/Services Page; Contact Us Page; About Us Page; Support Page and others. These primary pages on your website can move you forward.

Importantly, you must build or design your website with the mindset of your business users (customers, clients and enquiries); build the website to be users' friendly; make your business information easy to access by any user; build the website with responsible and responsive chat bolt or contact bolt; ensure to make your website to be better than other competitive websites to your business.

In building your mighty business to the best, you can outsource your website designing to the freelancer skillful in that aspect from the freelancer websites mentioned in the previous chapter.

If you build your website through any domain name registry or through a website designer from freelancer website or from someone else, you must ensure that the following factors are built in as the contents of your website:

1. Your business branding,
2. Easy transaction process with integration of trust,
3. Model your products or services with ease of payment on the website,
4. Power up your sales service on the website,
5. Make payment process easy on the website,
6. Keeping of customers/clients/ visitors data on the website for subsequent promotion on reaching out to them,
7. Provisions of your business social media on the website,
8. Ensuring sustainability of your website 24/7 with good hosting company,
9. Giveaways like free eBooks or downloadable videos of your products or services,
10. Ensure that adequate support service is integrated to

    the website,

11. Ensure your website will be built for optimum search engine keywords,

12. The website's content should have contents to educate your visitors,

13. If need be, ensure to design a community within the website where your customers or clients or visitors can ask questions and receive supports seamlessly,

14. Making your terms and conditions of engagements on website simple and straightforward,

15. Ensure that the policy of your website is clear and legal,

16. Ensure to comply with legal and ethical principles of your mighty business idea or inspiration on the websites and many other better factors you may factor in to building the website.

Summary and Biblical Illustrations

1. There are great benefits for your inspired business idea when you use website for your business. Have you ever considered the link between letters starting with God's concept of creation in the Holy Bible in John chapter 1 verse 1 which says, "In the beginning was the **Word**, and the **Word** was with God, and the **Word** was God." There is 'WWW' in the previous bible verse, if we connect it with God's mighty plan for mankind in Genesis chapter 1 verse 28 on 'having dominion' over the earth, you will see that your mighty business idea is the concept of God which is linked with having business website that will ensure that your business dominion is spread over the earth.

2. Imagine how you purchased this book, probably from amazon website or other website, and see the power of reaching out to you through this book. Without the help of the website, you might never benefit from my

book. So, without having website for your mighty inspiration which fuels your business idea to reach the uttermost part of the earth, you might not be able to have good success on the mighty idea.

3. Gone are the days of renting or leasing bricks and mortar warehouse or an office to do greatly in business. Although you may need a warehouse or an office but the potential of having a website for your business can't be washed down.

4. Having best website with the current state of the art in website designing shall make your business to be great if done right.

CHAPTER SIX

HOW TO GET MONEY TO GROW
YOUR ONLINE BUSINESS

Getting money for your mighty idea to start online business or grow your existing business doesn't have to be a rocket science. I have discussed in the previous chapters that if your inspiration is from the Almighty God, then He will support you with many assistances which will definitely required you taking actions pro-actively. I will like you to note what God says to Cyrus in the Holy Bible in the book of Isaiah chapter 45 verse 3 that, "...I will give thee the treasures of darkness, and hidden riches of secret places, that thou mayest know that I, the LORD, which call thee.." There are ways God will provide for you and supply your financial needs for your business, but you have to follow His instructions on each occasion in order to actualize His provisions for your business.

I read about a preacher who was inspired to purchase a large piece of land running to a hundred of hectares in a forest for the minis-try. The preacher was skeptical but knew that God instructed and directed him to do so. Today, the ministry of the Preacher on the same land he purchased then has gone far to look like a mini city.

There are different ways you can get money to finance your busi-ness but you must be led accordingly. I mean first thing first, seek God to whom He is leading you to. Nevertheless, if you check on-line how to get money for your business idea, you will see many guides. I will only list among the few I know but I hold on to my major opinion on seeking God's direction first.

The following are the highlights on some of the ways to get money to finance your business:

1. Your personal savings or income from your formal job is your starting capital for your business. I can tell you this savings or personal income, in most cases, is not always sufficient to accelerate your mighty business

growth successfully. I am not in the position to analyze how much you will need to start with or amount needed to move your already existing business forward. You may say, "I have no savings neither personal money to fall back to in order to kick start my business as I'm inspired." If that is true, you don't have to be discouraged. You can legally make personal money if you search your immediate environment for what you do in exchange for money. You can go online and sign up to some free websites that will allow you to do some works and make money.

2. Your family members and friends who believe in you and your inspired idea are the next channel from which money to finance your business can come from. What you need do is to let them understand in detail what your projection is all about and how you have planned to make good progress in the offing.

3. There some provisions for small business grants in the States in America and Governments of other Countries. I believe these grants may not be released to everyone, except there is proof of incorporation and business plan is clearly prepared. With your clear business plan, some have said that is the easiest to receive grants for your business with possibility of waiver of taxes (subject to your state requirements). Note that immediately you have made your request for the grant and if it is declined, you have to seek for other means.

4. Goal-Getter Investors' fund is another means of promoting or kicks starting your business. I mean, if you have found those investors or proactive business persons who see potentials in your mighty idea and how to move the idea to successful business, you should woo them to pool funds together with mutual understanding from your memorandum of Understanding on how to share profits or dividends from the business profits in future.

5. Do you have any used item in your house, garage, office or store that has been occupying space without any benefit to you? Such items like used old car parts, furniture, cartoons of empty bottles, used textbooks, used clothes, etc are potential sources of incomes for your business. I remember a story of a young man whose Dad died and he was trying to get rid of used old books of his Dad when he saw a perfect drawing of the former US President's picture. The young man was fascinated with the drawing, although with pencil, but perfectly drawn. The same drawn was auctioned by the man for $6,550! Are you surprised?! A paper meant to be dumped in waste trash became something of value to the young man. You may not know the financial potential of the abandoned used items you have if you do not try to dispose them off in exchange for funds for your business.

6. Your current job can be of help to help you save for launch or reinvest into your business growth. You may need to discipline yourself and minimize your expenses in order to save money for your business to kick start soon or to reinvest in your already existing business for growth.

7. Credit Card business financing is another opportunity you can explore for source to finance your business and make it grow. Personally, I don't like using credit card for business because of related issues associated with it if there is hitch your repayment plans.

8. Give license to use your mighty idea to potential users or business with iron clad legal documents to raise money. This method may work for you or not. Reasons are that your business may not have the capacity to be licensed to other person to us; your business idea may stolen and taken away from you; and your business secret or potential trade secret may be easily be used without adequate compensation. Some people have used the method and it worked for them, while others

couldn't find success in using it.

To this end, look around you to see another method to move your business forward to attain its full potentials.

Summary and Biblical Illustrations

1. The widow debt's was paid in the Holy Bible in the book of 2Kings chapter 4 by divine instructions. Here, you are not in debt but the concept from her story is that if you desire God's provision financially for your business, you need divine instructions on how to get money to finance your business idea.

2. Take time to go to search engine and see how the wealthy men in this country started with funding their business to build wealthy empires today. I like the histories of John Davison Rockefeller and Henry Ford who left wealthy legacy to their families through oil business and car manufacturing respectively.

3. Business with great potentials may face financial challenges from onset, but a determined inspired you will not let the financial challenges to dash off your visions and focus.

CHAPTER SEVEN

DETERMINATION AND PERSISTENCY HAVE THEIR DIVIDENDS ON ONLINE BUSINESS

I will not take much of your time in this chapter. I only want you to know that mighty inspiration births great reality when determination and tenacity of purpose are explored in achieving success in business.

You will need determination and persistency in decision making, spending, risk management, dealing with customers or clients, family pressure, meeting targets, legal constraints, regulatory controls, emotional and mental strains, meeting demands, overcoming competitions among plethora reasons which will come your way to tempt you to lose focus. Don't lose focus! Determination and persistency in the face of all these factors above shall strengthen you and give you huge dividends in the offing.

I will give you few biblical verses which are believed as inspirations of the Almighty that you have to look into at all time to encourage yourself in order to achieve great goals for your online business.

Biblical Doses for Determination and Persistency

1. **DON'T FAINT IN ADVERSITY**: If thou faint in the day of adversity, thy strength *is* small. (Proverbs 24 verse 10). No matter the challenges you may face in the cause of growing your business, don't faint at all. Esau lost his birthright t o Jacob in the Holy Bible because of temporary challenge and that affected him for years before he could found meaning to his life.

2. **BE DILIGENT:** To succeed in your business you must be diligent to see to how to grow your business and move

it higher. Holy Bible in the book of Proverbs chapter 22 verse 29 says, "Seest thou a man diligent in his business? He shall stand before kings; he shall not stand before mean man."

3. **HAVE RULE OVER YOUR DECISION**: To be a successful business person, you must be decisive in decision taking to help your business. Same Proverbs chapter 25 verse 28 says, "He that hath no rule over his own spirit is like a city that is broken down, and without walls." Proactive decision making in business saves many future pitfalls. And such proactive decision taking rests on the business owner who has strong rule over his or her spirit.

4. **INDECISION IS DANGERIOUS TO BUSINESS GROWTH**: To remain nonchalant in business world is a loss to any business operating in such realm. The book of Revelation chapter 3 verse 15 says, "...Because thou art lukewarm...I will spew thee out of my mouth."

5. **DOMINION COMES WITH WORKING**: You have to take your online business serious with hard work coupled with wisdom. The Bible reference of God's blessedness to mankind in Genesis chapter 1 verse 28 is to work on all the creations the Creator has made. You go very far successfully if you work on all you have to work on to make your online business a successful one.

6. **KEEP PRAYING**: This may sound uncommon in business world, but prayer works wonders for any wise man that sees need to pray for success in business and every aspect of life.

7. **WISDOM**: Bible says wisdom is the principal thing, therefore get wisdom, with all thy getting get understand. I will not over flog this point. But I will let you know that it is the key to good success.

8. **SEEK GOD ALWAYS**: There is one of the bible verses that I cherish much. That is the book of 2 Chronicles 26 verse 5, which states that, "And he sought God in the days of Zechariah, who had understanding in the visions of God: *and as long as he sought the LORD, God made him to prosper.*" To succeed in the online business and in every area of life, here lies a secret of good achievement in order to prosper in life.

CHAPTER EIGHT

PROTECT YOUR ONLINE BUSINESS INTELLECTUAL PROPERTY

Intellectual property of your business is one of the good assets of your business and it facilitates growth of business in all ramifications. An individual or business has commercial value or right of his intellectual inventions. I carefully searched for some biblical verses that are related to intellectual property, there isn't any direct reference from the Holy Bible. I actually found three bible verses which can be inferred to discuss briefly on intellectual property.

The first bible reference is the book of Matthew chapter 7 verse 6 which states, "Give not that which is holy unto the dogs, *neither cast ye your pearls before swine, lest they trample them under their feet, and turn again and rend you.*" Also, the book of Deuteronomy chapter 19 verse 14 states that, "You shall not remove *your neighbor's landmark*, which the men of old have set, in your *inheritance which you will inherit* in the land that the LORD your God is giving you to possess." In the case of Jacob in Genesis chapter 30 verse 40, the Holy Bible states that, "And Jacob did separate the lambs, and set the faces of the flocks toward the rings raked, and all the brown in the flock of Laban; and he put his own flocks by themselves, and put them not unto Laban's cattle." What Jacob did was example of trademark or trade secret that was difficult of Laban to claim right of ownership from Jacob.

These three verses actually indicate that you or your business has 'pearls' that have to be kept jealously, you and your neighbor have landmark which are your inheritances. By extension, you must protect your business intellectual property and you must desist from infringing on other person or business' intellectual property.

Availability of information and technological products around us has opened the world of business to challenges of intellectual property theft. Intellectual property has different classifications and relevancies in certain aspects of business or individual's work of invention or idea. These classifications include trademarks, copyrights, trade secret, patents and industrial designs.

There are two major government registries to register your intellectual property in USA depending on the classification of the intellectual property you want to register. To register a trademark or Patent invention, you can easily access the U.S. Patent and Trademark Office's Website, https://www.uspto.gov and explore the procedures for the registration. For the copyright's registration, go to the U.S. Copyright office's website, https://www.copyright.gov/. If you are outside the U.S., you can register in any government's office of your country.

The process of registrations of all your business intellectual properties can be perfectly be handled by a competent lawyer. If you decide to save cost, you can personally commence the process on any of the websites.

The other aspects of protecting your intellectual property are where you want to license or franchise your online business to other party. You have to ensure that every legal requirement is meant in order to secure your intellectual property associated with your online business. More also, it important to note that your legal documentation on licensing or franchising your online business must be made in such ways that third party's intellectual right is not infringed upon.

CHAPTER NINE

COMPLIANCE WITH BUSINESS
LAWS AND REGULATIONS

Anybody that establishes business in any society is required to abide by the legal principles and regulations of the society. In this chapter, I want you to learn the basic, but not exhaustive, laws, rules, ethics and regulations that will enhance your business success.

The bible references are 1 Peter chapter 2 verses 13-14 which provides that, "Submit yourselves for the Lord's sake to every human institution, whether to a king as the one in authority, or to governors as sent by him for the punishment of evildoers and the praise of those who do right." Titus chapter 3 verse 1 states that, "Remind them to be subject to rulers, to authorities, to be obedient, to be ready for every good deed," As the bible supports that everyone should subjects to and obey the authorities, your might idea and business inspired by the Almighty must be done in obedience to God, your state's government and constituted regulatory institutions related with your business.

Business Laws: These are set of laws that guide businesses in our country. These aspects of laws are related to business liability, contract laws, contract of employment law, law of torts, negligence, duty of cares, negotiable instruments, law of agency, sales of goods law, corporate governance law, law of banking and negotiable instruments, and many more. Your lawyer or online resource you choose will guide you through all these laws and ones that are relevant to your business idea.

Law of Taxation: Taxation is like life wire to financial functioning of our society and governments. Your business should set its taxation responsibilities right. Issue of taxation is as old as our country. When Jesus was asked in the bible on matter concerning taxes, Jesus said (in Mark chapter 12 verse 17), "And Jesus answering said unto them, Render to Caesar the things that are Caesar's, and to God the things that are God's. And they marveled at him."

Business Ethics: Every business or profession requires basic ethical principles to be observed or carried out in cause of relating with customer, clients, patient or others as the case may be. Business ethics is a set of principles that imperative to be observed in every business environment. I will not be able to accurately give you a set of ethics or codes for a particular business. But you have to find out what are the ethical principles that are relevant to your great business idea and set same to guide you, your team mangers and your prospective customers/clients/patient as the case may be.

Criminal Liability: You must ensure to carry out your business with due diligence to avoid criminal claims against your business because this will affect you personally. Criminal liability for an incorporated business entity is charged personally on the directors or shareholders of the business. These directors or shareholders are the mind and brain of the business entity. If a business is faced with many criminal liabilities, such may ruin the business.

Privacy Rights and Protection: This is very important for every business nowadays. Every business that operates both online and offline should ensure that the privacy policy of the business is made known to everyone relating with and outside the business. Government of every country has put legal measures in places to guide every business to imbibe the practice of setting privacy rights and protection policy. Failure to strictly comply with this aspect of business legal matter is dangerous to any business.

Alternative Disputes Resolution (ADR) Mechanisms: Disputes are indispensable in business environment. A good business promoter will always prefer to explore ADR mechanisms to resolve disputes as there arise in the business transactions and relations with everyone. ADR mechanisms are arbitration, negotiation, mediation, conciliation among others. I believe these mechanisms sustain goodwill of every business rather than litigations in law courts.

Summary and Biblical Illustrations

1. The book of Isaiah chapter 1 verse 19 says, "If ye be willing and obedient, ye shall eat the good of the land." To have good success for your business, obey and observe all laws, rules and regulations associated with your business.
2. Do everything in your power to ensure that your business comply with all legal principles, ethical codes and regulatory requirements for your business.
3. Endeavour to include ADR as means of resolving any disputes in your business documentations.

CHAPTER TEN

EXPAND YOUR ONLINE
BUSINESS GLOBALLY

Expansion of your business has been made easy with your business. But you must understand the concepts and factors that enhance global expansion of business. Like you know that the biblical injunction to mankind in Genesis chapter verse 28 is for all to be fruitful, multiply, replenish, and to take dominion of all the earth. You must have desire to take your inspired business global.

Note that global business expansion is not always the only good means of growing your business. The country consumptions and demands' rates are higher that any business start-up in U.S. will submit that the market is huge enough and there may be no reason to think of global expansion of business. In reality, anyone that projects to expand his/her business globally is embarking on huge challenge with huge potential profits in the offing. Therefore, if you desire to move or grow your business globally, I can say you have chosen great decision which I am confident in you that you will have good success in the business in the nearest future.

Let us consider the practicality of this global expansion of business. Can a law firm, a fashion designer, an author, online entrepreneur, farmer, etc go global in the businesses and services? The answer is yes. There are not required to be everywhere in the world but there businesses and services can be accessible anyway in the world through internet and other online resources to be discussed below.

Ways to Expand Your Business Globally

1. **Affiliate Marketing**: As we have discussed earlier that your business website is a great resource to grow your business. So, what is affiliate marketing? It is one of the benefits of selling one's products or services through an-

other person or business with aim that you will share the profit with the other person when he/she sells the products or services.

For example, Amazon has many persons who are selling goods and services of other persons through link to the goods and services on their various websites or blogs.

2. **Licensing**: You can license you business to other businesses or persons in other countries in the world. This process requires some legal documentations and advice. You, the licensor will give legal right to the licensees in the other countries to sell your products or manufacture your products in the other countries for agreed sum of fee or royalty.

The big companies like Coca-Cola, Toyota Motors, Amazon, etc are examples of companies or businesses that have expanded globally by the strength of licensing their products and services.

3. **Connect with Big E-Commerce Websites**: There are having big e-commerce websites more than decades now that have been making business owner of inspired ideas to grow globally. You can start your business from your home or office by connecting with any of these big e-commerce websites. Examples of these big websites are Amazon.com; shopify.com alibaba.com etc.

4. **Franchise Your Business**: Franchising in one of the tools to grow your business globally. That is, you enter into legal agreement with other person to sell your business somewhere else as if you are the same person selling the business in the other territories. We have examples of this arrangement around us.

5. **Utilize Outsourcing Mechanism**: This is a secret many people in business do not know till now. This mechanism is a good method you can use to expand your

business internationally. What does this mechanism entails? It is a method where a foreign business or company produces goods to other foreign business with private libeling right. The latter will brand the product as his/her products the country. Example is common with some companies in U.S. now outsource their goods from China and sell same goods here as if they produced them in the country. This mechanism has enhanced drop shipping businesses as well.

6. **Foreign Joint Venture and Foreign Subsidiaries**: You can expand your business globally by engaging foreigners in their various counties to incorporate your business in their domain with agreed terms and conditions.

Summary and Biblical Illustrations

1. With the above opportunities, you can move your business globally. But we have to bear it in mind that global expansions are prone to some challenges like cultural differences, different laws and regulation; religious factor; environmental factors, currency and exchange rate factors, political factors among others.
2. These challenges can be overcome gradually when you take the bull by the horn to grow your business globally.
3. The book of Zechariah chapter 4 verse 10 asks, "For who hath despised the day of small things?" You should not despise the opportunities in growing your business.

LEARN AND REINVEST PROFITS
FOR SUSTAINABILITY

In conclusion, I want to encourage you to develop yourself as a pro business person. You have to buy some books online or in the local book store around you to read more about businesses and new development around the globe that can enhance your online business.

Also, there are free online resources where you can learn new methods of doing business. For examples, udemy.com, teacheable.com, and some free online universities business courses can help you accelerate your business growth.

Above all, the bible says in the book of Joshua chapter 1 verse 8 that, "This book of the law shall not depart out of thy mouth; but thou shalt meditate therein day and night, that thou mayest observe to do according to all that is written therein: for then thou shalt make thy way prosperous, and then thou shalt have good success." It is very important to study the bible in order to explore the hidden riches in it that can help you grow your business successfully.

Please note, as you make profits and grow your business, ensure certain percentage of your business profit goes to other investments. Your business may be relevant today but if its products are no longer needed or competitors have reduced profit making in the future, your reinvestment in other related modern methods of doing the business right will help you.

Thank you for trading this book. I wish you good success in your business.

www.ingramcontent.com/pod-product-compliance
Lightning Source LLC
Chambersburg PA
CBHW030531220526
45463CB00007B/2792